The Twelve
APOSTLES

REV. JUDE WINKLER, OFM Conv.

Imprimi Potest: Michael Kolodziej, OFM Conv., Minister Provincial of St. Anthony of Padua Province (USA)
Nihil Obstat: Sr. Kathleen Flanagan, S.C., Ph.D., Censor Librorum
Imprimatur: ✠ Frank J. Rodimer, J.C.D., Bishop of Paterson

Jesus Chooses the Apostles

IN ancient times, God spoke to His people through the prophets and other messengers. They proclaimed what God wanted for His people and from His people. But the people would not listen to the prophets. They turned from God's ways and sinned.

Then, when the chosen time had arrived, God sent His own Son. Jesus was born in Bethlehem and grew up in Nazareth where He was cared for by Joseph and Mary.

When Jesus was around 30 years old, He left Nazareth to travel throughout Israel preaching the Good News. He proclaimed that the Kingdom of God was at hand.

The Kingdom of God was a way of saying that people would live in God's love. Jesus spoke about how God forgave us our sins and how we had to turn from those sins to live in justice and mercy.

Many people came to hear Jesus teach and to see the great miracles that He performed. Some of these people followed Him and became His disciples. Jesus chose twelve of those disciples to be His special companions and to continue His work after He had returned to His Father in heaven. These were the twelve apostles.

Saint Peter

June 29

THE head of the apostles was St. Peter. Peter first learned about Jesus through his brother Andrew. Then one day Peter was fishing with his brother in their father's boat. Jesus called him and he left his father's boat and followed Jesus.

Peter saw many great things. Jesus healed his mother-in-law from a terrible fever. He saw Jesus bring Jairus' daughter back to life. He was with Jesus when He appeared in glory on Mount Tabor during the Transfiguration.

The night that Jesus was arrested, Peter denied that he even knew Jesus. He was so sorry for this that he cried and cried. But Jesus forgave him.

After Jesus rose, He asked Peter three times whether he loved Him, giving Peter the chance to make up for his mistake. Jesus then made him the shepherd of the flock, His representative upon the earth.

Peter gave the greatest witness to his love when he died on the cross in Rome. As a sign of his humility, he asked to be put upside down on the cross for he felt he was not worthy to die the same way that Jesus did.

Saint Andrew

ANDREW was St. Peter's brother and a fisherman like him. He began to follow Jesus even before Peter did.

Andrew was originally a follower of St. John the Baptist. One day John the Baptist saw Jesus walking by, and he proclaimed to his listeners, "Behold, the lamb of God."

When Andrew and another disciple heard what John the Baptist had said, they followed Jesus and became His disciples. Andrew was so moved by what he saw and heard that he told his brother Peter about Jesus, saying that Jesus must be the Messiah.

Andrew continued to lead people to Jesus by his preaching the Gospel throughout the countries of the east, especially in Greece, Poland, and Russia. He is greatly loved in these countries, and he is given as much reverence in countries of the east as Peter is given in countries of the west.

Like Jesus and Peter, Andrew died on the cross, but the cross upon which he died was shaped more like an X than a T.

Saint James the Greater

July 25

THERE were two apostles named James. To tell them apart, one of them is called St. James the Greater and the other is called St. James the Lesser.

James the Greater was a fisherman like John, his brother, and Peter and Andrew. Like them, he left his father's boat and his work and followed Jesus. He did not really lose his work, though, for while he did not search for fish any more, he did become a "fisher of men."

James became one of the "three great apostles." Whenever Jesus did something important, He took three apostles with Him: Peter, James, and John. They were with Jesus when He raised Jairus' daughter from the dead, when He appeared in glory on Mount Tabor, and when He prayed in the Garden of Olives the night of Holy Thursday.

James preached the Gospel throughout Judea and Samaria. There is even a legend that he traveled as far away as Spain to proclaim the Good News. He was one of the first martyrs of the Church, for he died for the faith in 43 A.D., only about ten years after the birth of the Church.

Saint John

December 27

MANY of the apostles had nicknames. Peter was the rock, the two James were the greater and the lesser, and Thomas was the Doubter. John's nickname is the most meaningful, for he was called the Beloved.

John was a fisherman along with his brother James. Jesus called him to leave his work and his father's boat and to follow Him.

John was with Jesus along with Peter and James whenever Jesus was doing something very important.

At the Last Supper, John sat near Jesus and asked Jesus who would betray Him. He followed Jesus when He was arrested, and even stood under the cross, refusing to abandon Jesus when all of the other apostles ran away.

Because of this, Jesus entrusted His mother to John and John to His mother. John cared for the Blessed Virgin Mary for the rest of her life here on earth until the day that she was taken up into heaven body and soul.

John wrote a Gospel, three letters, and the Book of Revelation to proclaim the Good News. Toward the end of his life, he was sent to the island of Patmos as a punishment for being a Christian.

Saint Philip

May 3

PHILIP was one of the first apostles. Jesus simply said to him, "Follow Me," and Philip left what he was doing and followed Jesus. He immediately called his friend Nathanael and told him that they had found the one whom Moses and the prophets had foretold.

Philip's faith was not always perfect. When Jesus multiplied the fish and bread for 5,000 people, He questioned Philip as to what He should do. Philip did not yet understand how powerful Jesus was and so he answered that even two-hundred-day's wages could not buy enough food for all 5,000. Jesus taught Philip about His power by multiplying the five pieces of bread and the two fish so that there was enough food for all of the people.

Later on, Philip showed his faith by bringing some people who were from Greece to Jesus so that they could hear Him teach. He wanted to share the most important thing that he had found in his life: his faith in Jesus.

Philip preached the Gospel throughout the area that is now the country of Turkey. He died for the faith there around 80 A.D.

Saint Bartholomew

August 24

THERE are some apostles about whom we know very little. St. Bartholomew is one of these.

In the Gospel of John, Bartholomew appears with a different name: Nathanael. It was not strange for people to have two names in those days. Simon was also known as Peter and Saul as Paul. Bartholomew was also Nathanael.

Philip called Nathanael and told him about Jesus. Nathanael had spent his life studying the law and the prophets and he could not believe that Jesus was the Messiah. Jesus was from Nazareth, a very poor town. Nathanael thought that the Messiah would be a rich king.

Jesus revealed Who He was to Nathanael by telling him that He saw him under the fig tree. That is where Jewish people would study the Bible, and Jesus was telling Nathanael that He was the One about Whom Nathanael had been reading. Jesus also promised Nathanael that he would see even greater things.

Bartholomew (Nathanael) was a missionary in Arabia and Turkey and India. He died for the faith in the country of Armenia, the first kingdom in the world to become Christian.

Saint Matthew

September 21

MATTHEW is very unusual, for he was not a fisherman or a student of the Bible when Jesus called him. He was a tax collector.

Jewish people hated tax collectors at the time of Jesus. They were collecting taxes for the Romans, the enemies of the Jews. They also often cheated people. Jewish people had nothing to do with them and would never think of eating with them.

Jesus called Matthew to come follow Him. He then went to Matthew's house for supper with him and his friends. The Jewish leaders were angry with Jesus for doing this. They thought that it was terrible that He would eat with such people. But Jesus told them that these were the people He had come to serve, for they were broken and needed His healing.

Matthew later wrote a Gospel to show how Jesus was the true Messiah. That is why he begins the Gospel by telling us the names of all of Jesus' ancestors all the way back to Abraham, the father of the Jews.

Tradition tells us that Matthew traveled to Ethiopia to preach the Gospel.

Saint Thomas

July 3

NOT everyone finds it easy to have faith. Thomas is one of those who struggled to believe.

When Jesus heard that His friend Lazarus was ill and that they should go to Jerusalem, Thomas said that all the disciples should follow Jesus to die with Him. But Thomas' courage was more words than deeds, for he ran away with the others when Jesus died on the cross.

Later, when Jesus rose from the dead and appeared to the disciples, Thomas was not present. When the disciples told Thomas that Jesus had risen, he would not believe them. He said that he wanted to be able to touch the wounds in Jesus' hands and side before he would believe.

The next Sunday, Jesus appeared to them and told Thomas that he could touch His wounds. Thomas responded by saying, "My Lord and My God."

This reminds us that we will not always understand everything, but we have to believe. An example of this is the Holy Eucharist. It looks like bread and wine, but we believe that it is the Body and Blood of Jesus.

Thomas preached in Persia and India where he died for the faith.

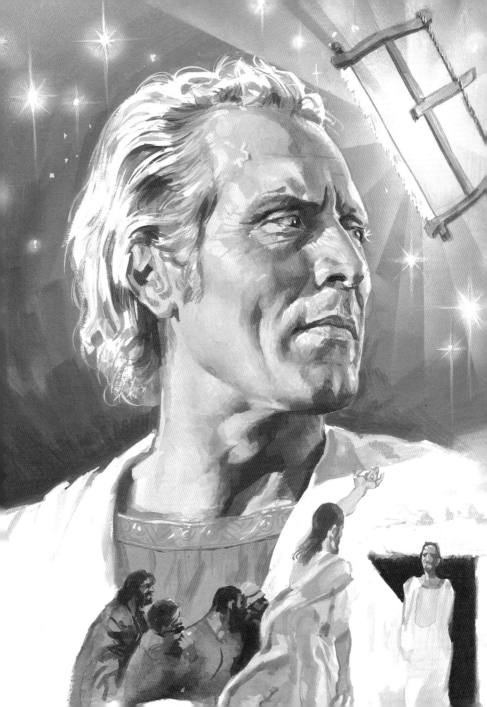

Saint James the Lesser

May 3

THERE are two apostles named James. To tell them apart, one is called James the Greater and the other is called James the Lesser. We already saw James the Greater. He was the brother of John and one of the three great apostles.

James the Lesser was a cousin of Jesus and the brother of the apostle Jude (and possibly a relative of Simon the Zealot).

After the Ascension, James became the leader of the Christian community in Jerusalem. There he helped to shape the direction that the early Church would take.

Later, when he wrote a letter to believers throughout the world, he spoke about the importance of putting our faith into action. It is not enough to feel bad for people who have nothing to eat—we have to do something for them so that they do not go hungry.

He also warned people about the danger of gossiping. Things we say can really hurt others. When we spread stories (even if they are true), we can crush a person's spirit.

James died for the faith in Jerusalem around the year 42 A.D.

Saint Simon the Zealot

October 28

AT the time of Jesus, there was a group of Jews in Israel who wanted to fight for their freedom. The Romans had conquered Israel and ruled it with great cruelty. These Jews fought against the Romans and were called Zealots.

One of these Zealots was a man named Simon. He became a follower of Jesus. We do not know much about him other than the fact that he was a relative of Jesus and James and Jude.

The Zealots and many of the Jews thought that Jesus was going to be the Messiah who would defeat the Romans. But Jesus did not come to establish a kingdom here on earth. His kingdom was not of this world.

Jesus came to preach the Good News that God's Kingdom was already dawning on the earth. God's Kingdom is about justice and mercy and love.

Even if in the beginning Simon might have followed Jesus for the wrong reason, he learned what Jesus meant at the cross and resurrection and especially when the Holy Spirit descended upon him and the other apostles and Mary on Pentecost Sunday.

Simon preached the Gospel in Arabia and Persia where he died as a martyr for the faith.

Saint Jude Thaddeus

October 28

IN many ways, St. Jude is more famous today than he was when he first began his preaching.

Jude was a brother of James the Lesser and most probably a cousin of Jesus (as well as being a relative of Simon the Zealot).

One of the letters of the New Testament was written by Jude. He warned people to be careful not to listen to false ideas about the faith. He said that some people spent all their time thinking up new, strange ideas. They were confusing good people and leading them astray.

Yet, Jude tells his readers to be gentle with those who make mistakes. He realized that love brings many more people to Christ than anger.

Jude preached the Gospel in Arabia with Simon and died for the faith in Persia along with him.

St. Jude is now known as the Patron Saint of hopeless causes. People all over the world ask for his intercession when they feel that they have no one else to whom they can turn. They feel great comfort in the fact that they have a friend who prays with and for them.

Judas Iscariot

OF the original twelve apostles, eleven of them are Saints. Only one of them, Judas, is not. He is the one who betrayed Jesus.

Why did Jesus choose Judas as an apostle? Maybe because Jesus always gave people a chance to turn from their sins and choose life.

But for some reason Judas did not want to choose that life. He went to the high priest and offered to betray Jesus for thirty pieces of silver.

Judas received his opportunity on Holy Thursday, the night of the Last Supper. During the meal, Jesus predicted that Judas would betray Him. After the meal Jesus went to the Garden of Olives to pray. Judas found Him there and greeted Him with a kiss, giving a sign to the temple guards that they should arrest Him. They seized Jesus and took Him away.

Even now, God would have forgiven Judas for this terrible sin. But Judas refused to ask for that forgiveness. He threw the money that he had received for betraying Jesus at the high priest's feet. Then Judas went out and killed himself.

Saint Matthias

May 14

AFTER Judas died, there were only eleven apostles left. The eleven met in the upper room where they had eaten the Last Supper and discussed what they should do.

St. Peter spoke to the others and said that they should choose another disciple to take Judas' place. There had to be twelve, because this was a special number for the people of Israel. There were twelve tribes and twelve patriarchs who were the founders of those twelve tribes. Now, Jesus had established a new Israel, the Church. There had to be twelve apostles for the new Israel.

The new apostle was to be someone who followed Jesus from the time of His Baptism by John the Baptist until the day that He ascended into heaven. There were two possibilities: Justus and Matthias.

The apostles left the choice to the Holy Spirit. They prayed and then had Justus and Matthias pick lots. The choice fell to Matthias who became the twelfth apostle.

Matthias preached in Judea and then in Ethiopia where he gave up his life for the faith.

Saint Paul

June 29

How many apostles were there? We have seen that Jesus chose twelve of His disciples to be the apostles, the leaders of the New Israel.

But St. Paul had a different idea of what it meant to be an apostle. He said that anyone who gave witness to the resurrection of Jesus was an apostle.

Paul never followed Jesus before the ascension. In fact, he even persecuted the early Christians. But then, while Paul was traveling to Damascus to arrest some Christians, Jesus appeared to him and called him to be the apostle to the pagans.

This changed Paul's life. From then on, he lived only for Jesus and the Good News. He traveled throughout the countries of the Middle East and Greece and even Rome to proclaim how much God loves us. He wrote many letters to encourage Christians in their faith. He suffered greatly for that faith, but he never wavered.

Then, around 67 A.D., Paul died for the faith in Rome. This was right around the same time that St. Peter died for the faith in Rome.

Prayer

LORD God, You called the apostles to share the Good News of Your love wherever they went. They risked everything they had, even their lives, to follow that call.

You have now called us to be servants of Your love. It is not always easy to be a Christian in today's world, so we need Your help.

Give us the courage to bear witness to our faith in our everyday lives: at home, at school, when we play, and when we work. Teach us to be witnesses to Your truth and love with whomever we meet today.

We ask this through Christ our Lord. Amen.